TIME FOR KIDS®

DEVELOPING 2 READER *Science Scoops*

Planets!

By the Editors of TIME FOR KIDS
WITH LISA JO RUDY

HarperCollinsPublishers

About the Author: Lisa Jo Rudy writes about science, technology, history, and social studies for kids. She helps to create exhibits, planetarium shows, hands-on kits, and educational materials. She is also the author of the TIME FOR KIDS® Science Scoops book *SNAKES!* Lisa Jo Rudy lives in Pennsylvania with her husband and two children.

For Sara, who can fly—and can't wait to bounce on the moon.

Special thanks to Bill Arnett, creator of the awe-inspiring www.nineplanets.org.   –L.J.R.

Library of Congress Cataloging-in-Publication Data is available.

ISBN 0-06-078202-1 (pbk.) — ISBN 0-06-078203-X (trade)

1 2 3 4 5 6 7 8 9 10
First Edition

Photography and Illustration Credits:
Cover: NASA; cover insert: NASA; cover flap: JPL/NASA; title page: NASA; contents page: Cornell/JPL/NASA; pp. 4–5: Gabe Palmer—Corbis; pp. 6–7: MSFC/NASA; pp. 8–9: Jean Tuttle: pp. 10–11; Northwestern University/JPL/NASA; pg. 11 (inset): JPL/NASA; pp. 12–13: NASA; pg. 12 (inset): JPL/NASA; pg. 13 (inset): John Courtney; pp. 14–15: Matthias Breiter—Minden; pg. 14 (inset): GSFC/NASA; pp. 16–17: JPL/NASA; pg. 16 (inset): NASA; pg. 17 (inset): JPL/NASA; pp. 18–19: JPL/NASA; pg. 19 (inset): NASA; pp. 20–21: University of Colorado/JPL/NASA; pg. 20 (inset): NASA; pg. 21 (inset): NASA; pp. 22–23: JPL/NASA; pg. 22 (inset): NASA; pp. 24–25: NASA; pg. 25 (inset): Lowell Observatory; pp. 26–27: B. Magrath—Photo Researchers; pp. 28–29: NASA; pg. 28 (inset): NASA & The Hubble Heritage Team (STScI/AURA); pg. 29 (inset): NASA; pp. 30–31: Seth Shostak—SETI Institute; pg. 31 (inset): NASA; pg. 32 (atmosphere): Matthias Breiter—Minden; pg. 32 (galaxy): MSFC/NASA; pg. 32 (orbit): Jean Tuttle; pg. 32 (planet): NASA; pg. 32 (solar system): Jean Tuttle; pg. 32 (universe): MSFC/NASA; pg. 32 (fun fact): John Courtney

Acknowledgments:
For TIME FOR KIDS: Editorial Director: Keith Garton; Editor: Nelida Gonzalez Cutler; Art Director: Rachel Smith; Photography Editor: Jill Tatara

go **Check us out at www.timeforkids.com**

CONTENTS

The surface
of Mars

CHAPTER ONE

Our Place in

Space

Look up into the night sky.
You can see the moon.
Soon the stars will shine.
They are all part of the universe.
The universe includes everything
that exists!

The universe has billions of stars.

A group of stars is called a galaxy.
There are billions of galaxies
in the universe.
Our sun is a star in the Milky Way galaxy.

The Milky
Way galaxy

Take a trip around our solar system.

Nine planets circle, or orbit, the sun.
The inner planets are made mostly of rock.
The outer planets, except Pluto, are made
mostly of gas.

Mercury
The daylight side of
Mercury is very hot.
It is freezing cold
on the dark side!

Earth
Our planet is medium size.
Four planets are larger.
Four planets are smaller.

Sun
The sun is a huge,
fiery ball of gas.

Venus
Venus is sometimes
mistaken for a star.
You may know it as
the "morning star"
or the "evening star."

Mars
The red planet
is a lot like Earth.
Scientists believe
it once had water
and flowing streams.

Jupiter
Jupiter is the largest planet.
All of the other planets
could fit inside it!

Saturn
Saturn is a cloud
of swirling gas.
Scientists think it may
have a rocky core.

Uranus
Uranus has at least
twenty-seven moons
and eleven rings.

Neptune
Sometimes Neptune's path
takes it even farther from
the sun than Pluto.

Pluto
Pluto is the smallest
and coldest planet.
It has one moon
called Charon.

CHAPTER TWO

Visit the Inner Planets!

Mercury's
surface

Mercury's surface has deep holes. It also has wide, flat plains. The days and nights are very long on Mercury. One full day takes two Earth months!

Venus's surface

Venus is covered in thick clouds.

Under the clouds are canyons and plains.
Venus also has sand dunes and mountains.

How Hot?

Venus is the hottest planet.
The planet's thick clouds trap the sun's heat.
The temperature reaches 800° to 900° F.
A fire on Earth is only 500° F!

Earth's surface

Earth has water, oxygen, and an atmosphere.

Atmosphere is the envelope of gas around a planet.
Earth's atmosphere protects us from the sun's rays.
Earth is the only planet in our solar system that can support life as we know it.

The dust and rock on Mars are rich in iron.

That is why the planet looks red.
Ice covers the poles of Mars.
The ice is made
of frozen gas.

How Big?

Olympus Mons is a mountain on Mars.
Its base is as wide as the state of Missouri.
The mountain is about sixteen miles high.
That's three times taller than Mount Everest,
the tallest mountain on Earth!

CHAPTER THREE

Voyage to the

Jupiter's
surface

Outer Planets

Jupiter is mostly just a big ball of gas! The planet's swirls and bands are clouds. Jupiter has at least sixty-three moons. Ganymede is the biggest. It is bigger than Mercury or Pluto.

Ganymede

Saturn has at least seven rings.

They are made of ice, rock, and dirt.
These bright rings reflect the sun's light.
Saturn also has at least thirty-one moons.
The moon Titan even has
frozen water and
an atmosphere.

Saturn's
rings

Titan

Uranus and Neptune look blue from Earth.

But they are streaked with colors.
Neptune and Uranus also have
thin, faint rings.
High winds blow huge storms
through their clouds.

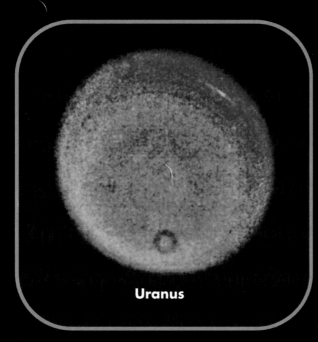

Uranus

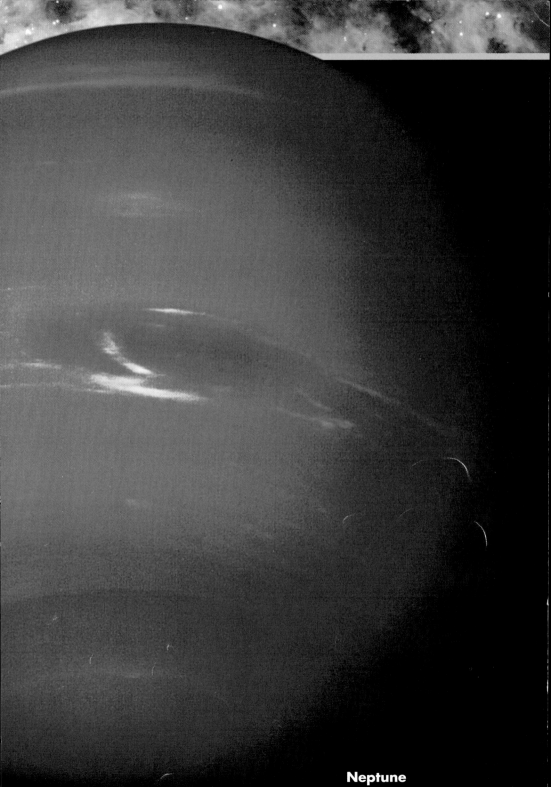

Neptune

Pluto

Pluto's moon,
Charon

Pluto is a tiny chunk of rock.

It is even smaller than Earth's moon!
So is Pluto really a planet?
Scientists still debate this question.

Spotlight

Pluto was discovered in 1930.
The scientists named it Planet X.
An eleven-year-old girl in England
had a better name.
Venetia Burney called the planet Pluto.
Pluto was the Greek god of
the underworld.
The scientists liked Venetia's idea!
They officially named the planet Pluto.

CHAPTER FOUR

Exploring Space

The Maunakea
Observatories
in Hawaii

Space scientists called astronomers use telescopes to view the universe. They also send spacecraft to get close-up views of the other planets. Astronomers hope to learn more about Earth this way.

Telescopes are our eyes on the sky.

There are four giant space telescopes.
One is the Hubble Space Telescope.
It has orbited Earth since 1990.

Hubble has sent back thousands of images.
There are pictures of stars being born,
distant galaxies, and sharp views of the planets.
These snapshots of space are amazing!

The Sombrero galaxy

Stars being born in
the Eagle Nebulae

The Hubble
Space Telescope

Is there anybody out there?

Some scientists are searching for alien life.
Their telescopes can see and hear into space.
Scientists are sending messages, too.
Will they get an answer?

The Allen Telescopes
in California

**Jupiter's Great
Red Spot**

Did You Know?

★ Our solar system is about
4,500,000,000 years old.

★ It takes Mercury only
eighty-eight days to travel
around the sun.

★ Winds blow at Saturn's
equator at 1,100 miles per hour.

★ Through a telescope, you can
see a storm on Jupiter.
It is called the Great Red Spot.
The giant storm is twice as big
as Earth.

WORDS to Know

Atmosphere:
an envelope of gas around a planet

Planet:
a ball-shaped lump of rock, gas, and metal that revolves around a star

Galaxy:
a group of billions of stars

Solar System:
a star with a group of objects that orbit it

Orbit:
a path around an object in space

Universe:
everything that exists anywhere

FUN FACT

Pluto is 3.5 billion miles away from Earth.
If you traveled at 600 miles per hour,
it would take you 690 years to get to Pluto!